Introduction

In the hectic few months before a wedding, it's easy to overlook how you're going to feel right after the event. After all, you've spent months (and possibly years) planning and preparing for your one big day in fine detail. Meanwhile, your friends and family are concentrating on the big picture—your long-term future as a couple. So how you're going to spend the two or three weeks immediately after your wedding day may feel like a secondary consideration. Don't let it. Make this the trip of a lifetime and a great way to start your married life.

In this Journal you'll find suggestions for where to go and plenty of practical hints and tips for organizing your trip. There's also space for you to record memories of your wedding, special details of your honeymoon, and plans for your first year together. Your completed Journal will become a touching portrait of the two of you at a special time in your lives. Take time to fill in the Honeymoon Diary—there are lined pages for your thoughts and plain "scrapbook" pages for sketches and jottings. And when you're back home, print your best pictures to go on the acid-free photo pages in the Honeymoon Photos section.

Have a wonderful honeymoon!

Where to...

Spot the Big Five (rhino, elephant, lion, leopard, and buffalo)
> game parks in southern Africa

Enjoy a car-free vacation
> Venice, Italy, where residents walk or go by canal on a vaporetto

View the northern lights
> around the North Pole. Canada, Iceland, or northern Norway are closer alternatives

Climb a mountain
> the Canadian Rockies; the Peruvian Andes; Mount Kilimanjaro, Tanzania

Dance all night
> Rio de Janeiro, Brazil, at the world's greatest carnival

Try your luck
> Las Vegas, Nevada, gambling capital of the United States

Open a bottle of bubbly
> the Champagne region of northern France, home of the famous drink

Watch the sun rise
> from the summit of Mount Fuji, Japan, in summer

Watch the sun set
> over Ayers Rock (Uluru), Australia, and watch the colors of the rock change

Get the gift of the gab
> Blarney Castle, Ireland. Kiss the Blarney Stone and receive the gift of eloquence

Window shop
> Fifth Avenue, New York City; Bond Street, London; the Champs Elysées, Paris

Sip a cocktail
> the bar at Raffles Hotel in Singapore, birthplace of the Singapore Sling

Be inspired by architectural beauty
> the Taj Mahal, Agra, India, built in memory of a beloved wife

Feel small
> next to a 300-foot (90-meter) redwood tree in California, in the Redwood State Parks

Ask for advice
> Delphi, Greece, the site of the famous oracle

Where shall we go?

Our shortlist of possible honeymoon destinations

Where shall we go?

Our shortlist of possible honeymoon destinations

Packing master list

Essentials

- [ ] Passport and necessary visas
- [ ] Vaccination certificates
- [ ] Tickets and travel arrangements
- [ ] Cash
- [ ] Credit cards
- [ ] Travel insurance details
- [ ] Address book or address labels
- [ ] Guidebook and phrasebook
- [ ] Camera and spare memory card
- [ ] Sunglasses and sunhat
- [ ] Spare prescription glasses, if needed
- [ ] Travel alarm clock

For the journey

- [ ] Bottled water
- [ ] Earplugs
- [ ] Sleep mask
- [ ] Neck pillow
- [ ] Lightweight warm sweater
- [ ] Compression socks for flying
- [ ] Books and magazines
- [ ] Magnetic travel games
- [ ] Hard candy (boiled sweets)
- [ ] Toothbrush and toothpaste

Medicine cabinet

- [ ] Any medication you take regularly and enough to cover your trip
- [ ] Painkillers
- [ ] Cold and cough remedy
- [ ] Antiseptic cream
- [ ] Antiseptic wipes
- [ ] Band-Aids
- [ ] Insect repellent
- [ ] Insect bite relief
- [ ] Anti-malarial medication, if appropriate
- [ ] Diarrhea relief
- [ ] Antihistamines, if you are allergic
- [ ] Sleeping pills
- [ ] Sun protection
- [ ] Aftersun
- [ ] Contraceptives
- [ ] Jetlag remedy
- [ ] Sanitary protection
- [ ] Gel handwash
- [ ] Wet wipes

Clothing and daily needs

- ❑ Comfortable clothes for sightseeing
- ❑ Jeans and casual wear
- ❑ Underwear
- ❑ Beach wear
- ❑ Evening wear
- ❑ Nightclothes
- ❑ Shoes and sandals
- ❑ Waterproof jacket
- ❑ Warm jacket, hat, gloves, and scarf for cold countries
- ❑ Wide-brimmed hat and loose cotton outfit for hot countries
- ❑ Toiletries
- ❑ Makeup and hairbrush

Luxuries

- ❑ Video camera
- ❑ Travel iron and adapter plug
- ❑ Hairdryer and adapter plug
- ❑ Hairstyling appliances
- ❑ MP3 player and portable dock or speakers
- ❑ Short-wave radio
- ❑ Scented travel candle
- ❑ Jewelry
- ❑ Perfume

Useful extras

- ❑ Cell phone
- ❑ Notepad
- ❑ Sketchbook
- ❑ Flashlight
- ❑ Swiss Army or other multitool knife
- ❑ Plastic ziplock bags
- ❑ Spare batteries and memory cards
- ❑ Umbrella
- ❑ Mosquito net
- ❑ Plug-in mosquito repeller or mosquito coils
- ❑ Calculator or currency convertor
- ❑ Playing cards
- ❑ Handkerchiefs

Packing list for her

Packing list for him

Packing and travel tips

- A suitcase with wheels helps to prevent an aching back and shoulders.
- On a long flight planes can get chilly, so wear something warm and loose-fitting. Take off your shoes and drink lots of water.
- A hard case gives contents the best protection.
- Pack heavy items in the bottom of your case.
- Put your washbag in a plastic bag in case of leaks, and decant toiletries into plastic travel bottles.
- Roll up T-shirts, socks, swimwear, and underwear and use them to cushion delicate items.
- Take clothes in a limited color palette so you can mix and match. Fabrics with Lycra travel well.
- Hang crumpled clothes in the bathroom, where the steam helps creases to drop out.

Honeymoon beauty wisdom

- Drink lots of water to prevent dehydration on the plane, and go easy on alcohol.

- Wear sun protection with an SPF of at least 15 (look for high UVA and UVB protection). Don't forget lips, eyes, and ears. Reapply suncream liberally every couple of hours.

- If you're pale, use a self-tanner and don't risk burning. Exfoliate and moisturize the skin before use, especially dry areas.

- Use alcohol-free perfume in the sun. Other perfumes may change their smell and cause skin irritation.

- Take a rich conditioner to prevent your hair from becoming dry in sun, sea, and chlorinated pools.

- Use plenty of moisturizer and aftersun lotion to rehydrate the skin.

- Useful makeup includes waterproof mascara, bronzing powder, and lipstick with sunscreen.

Checklist: Before we go

- ❏ Make sure your passport will be valid for at least six months at the time of your trip, and arrange any necessary visas and travel permits. Allow plenty of time for this if you're going off the tourist track. Make sure the name on tickets and passports match—this usually means booking in the wife's maiden name, unless you are going to apply for a new passport before you marry.

- ❏ Make photocopies of important documents—including passport, driver's license, and travel insurance policy—and leave a set with a responsible person at home.

- ❏ Take another set of photocopies with you and keep them separate from the originals in your luggage.

- ❏ Make an itinerary of your honeymoon and leave it with family or friends. If you are going on an extended trip, consider setting up your own web page or blog to keep everyone updated.

- ❏ Arrange comprehensive travel insurance and check that it offers appropriate cover for your trip, especially sports and adventure activities.

- ❏ Citizens of European Union countries traveling in certain European countries need to apply for a European Health Insurance Card entitling them to reciprocal medical care not covered by insurance.

- ❏ See your doctor for a medical and for advice if you're going to a high-altitude country or are planning on scuba-diving, long-distance trekking, or taking part in any hazardous sports.

- ❏ Find out if you need any vaccinations for the country or countries you're visiting. Do this eight weeks before you depart; some vaccinations require a follow-up visit.

- ❏ If you are taking any medication with you, carry it in your hand luggage and take a copy of the prescription along in case you lose your medicine, with a doctor's letter.

- ❏ If you have booked any part of your trip online, make sure you have noted down all the necessary reference numbers for your booking, plus a phone number to call for enquiries.

- ❏ Make sure you have enough money for your trip, plus extra funds for emergencies. It is a good idea to carry more than one source, for example credit cards and cash.

- ❏ If possible, buy some currency of the country you're visiting in advance.

- ❏ Carry a list of embassies or consular offices in the countries you are visiting.

- ❏ If you're going to send postcards or letters home, print recipients' details onto adhesive address labels, to save you time when you're away.

- ❏ Cancel your regular newspaper and other deliveries, and arrange for your pets to be cared for while you're away. Ask a neighbor to water your plants and check that mail doesn't pile up on your doorstep.

- ❏ If you're taking a cell phone with you, check its international coverage, and what the charges will be.

- ❏ Buy a reputable travel guide to your destination, to help you make the most of your trip. Prepare yourself by finding out about local habits and customs, from tipping to modes of dress when visiting religious sites.

- ❏ Pack a phrasebook of the country you're visiting—it could help in an emergency.

Notes

Notes

Notes

Before we go

Notes

Our trip

A photograph of us at our wedding

Our hotel

Our hotel

Places we visited

Places we visited

Places we visited

Places we visited

Special meals and nights out

Special meals and nights out

Special meals and nights out

Special meals and nights out

Sports and activities we tried

Sports and activities we tried

Sports and activities we tried

Sports and activities we tried

Books we read

Books we read

Our playlist

Our playlist

Notes

Notes

Notes

Notes

Honeymoon diary

Memories are made of this...

Memories of our wedding—her

Memories of our wedding—her

Memories of our wedding—her

Memories of our wedding—her

Memories of our wedding—him

Memories of our wedding—him

Memories of our wedding—him

Memories of our wedding—him

When we're back

- Finish writing any outstanding thank-you letters.
- Make sure all bills relating to the wedding are settled and check any rented formalwear has been returned.
- Clean and store the bride's dress and other special clothing.
- Arrange delivery of gift list items, if not already done.
- If the bride is changing her surname, inform all relevant organizations and apply for new bank cards, driver's license, and other documentation.
- Make new wills, if not already done.
- Make our selection of wedding photographs and have prints made.
- Compile wedding photo albums.
- Edit our wedding video.
- Send wedding cake to those who couldn't attend.
- Update our website.

When we're back

Honeymoon diary

Honeymoon diary

Honeymoon diary

Honeymoon diary

Honeymoon diary

Honeymoon diary

Honeymoon diary

Honeymoon diary

Honeymoon diary

Honeymoon diary

Honeymoon diary

Honeymoon diary

Honeymoon diary

Honeymoon diary

Honeymoon diary

Honeymoon diary

Honeymoon diary

Honeymoon diary

Honeymoon diary

Plans for our first year together—her

Plans for our first year together—her

Plans for our first year together—her

Plans for our first year together—her

Plans for our first year together—him

Plans for our first year together—him

Plans for our first year together—him

Plans for our first year together—him

Honeymoon photos

Photography credits

Caroline Arber Pages 3, 68 & 111/designed and made by Jane Cassini and Ann Brownfield

Jan Baldwin Front jacket, pages 8, 41, 50, 71, 92, 95, 143

Carolyn Barber Pages 53, 54, 58

Martin Brigdale Back jacket, pages 25, 37

Peter Cassidy Pages 30, 83, 87

Christopher Drake Pages 24, 35, 36, 49, 51, 79

Dan Duchars Page 42

Daniel Farmer Page 11

Winfried Heinze Pages 4, 5, 12, 17, 20, 28, 45, 46, 64, 67, 107

Paul Massey Pages 7, 32, 84

James Merrell Pages 9, 80

David Montgomery Pages 29, 75, 91

Kristin Perers Pages 14, 15, 19, 109

Claire Richardson Pages 1, 13, 16, 23, 96

Chris Tubbs Pages 72, 76/Giorgio and Ilaria Miani's Podere Casellacce in Val d'Orcia—available to let: ilariamiani@tin.it, 100/Marina Ferrara Pignatelli's home in Val d'Orcia, Tuscany

Simon Upton Pages 2 & 31/De Yturbe Arquitectos—www.deyturbe.com, 38

Ian Wallace Page 144

Polly Wreford Pages 57, 61, 63, 88, 99, 103, 104, 110

Designer Barbara Zuñiga
Picture Research Emily Westlake
Production Ros Holmes
Art Director Leslie Harrington
Publishing Director Alison Starling

First published in the UK in 2010
by **Ryland Peters & Small**
20–21 Jockey's Fields
London WC1R 4BW

and in the USA
by **Ryland Peters & Small, Inc.**,
519 Broadway, 5th Floor
New York, NY 10012

www.rylandpeters.com

ISBN 978-1-84597-923-2

Printed in China